The Big Book of Buildings

Written by Jon Richards

Illustrated by David Leeks

BRIMAX

Contents

Introduction

Take a look at the world around you and you will see that it is filled with buildings. There are buildings that we live in, buildings that we go to work or school in, and buildings that we just travel through. There are small homes and huge castles, as well as ornate temples and plain industrial buildings.

This book will show you a wide range of buildings, from churches to palaces, and from airports to homes. Each topic is explained simply and supported by bright illustrations, amazing facts, and easy-to-understand descriptions of these super structures.

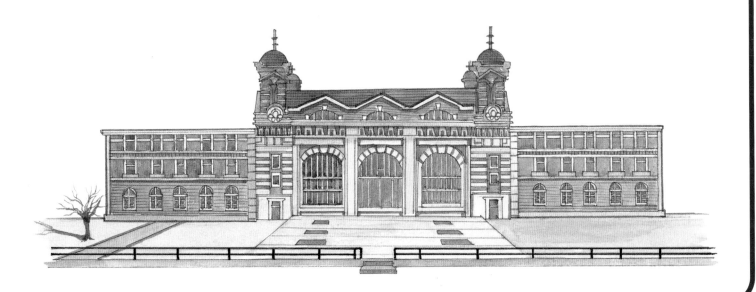

Mighty monuments

Monuments are built to celebrate events, such as battles, anniversaries, or the lives of famous people. They are built to be noticed and are usually very big or richly decorated with jewels or engravings.

Seven wonders of the ancient world

The seven wonders of the ancient world were considered to be the greatest monuments of ancient times. These seven wonders were the Pyramids at Giza in Egypt, the Hanging Gardens of Babylon, the Temple of Artemis at Ephesus, the Statue of Zeus at Olympia, the lighthouse on the island of Pharos, the Mausoleum of Halicarnassus, and the Colossus of Rhodes, which was a bronze statue that stood 30 m. (100 ft.) above the port of Rhodes in Greece.

Colossus of Rhodes

Mexican pyramid

The massive Pyramid of the Sun stands in the ruined city of Teotihuacan in Mexico. Little is known about the people who built it, but it is 66 m. (216 ft.) high and 230 m. (760 ft.) wide.

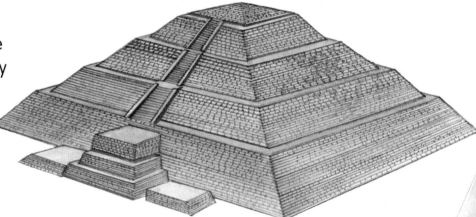

Taj Mahal

The Taj Mahal in India was built to hold the body of the wife of an emperor. This beautiful building is decorated with crystal and lapis lazuli, which is a semi-precious stone.

The Arc de Triomphe is 50 m. (166 ft.) high.

Arc de Triomphe

The Arc de Triomphe in Paris, France, was built by the Emperor Napoleon to celebrate his own military victories. It was started in 1806, but took another 30 years to complete.

The elevators in the Eiffel Tower travel over 100,000 km. (62,500 miles) every year.

Did you know?

The Eiffel Tower was never meant to be a permanent structure. It was supposed to be taken apart a few years after its completion.

Gateway to the West

This huge arch in St. Louis, Missouri, USA, was built to celebrate the historic role of the city as the "gateway to the west". It is made from stainless steel and is 192 m. (630 ft.) high.

Eiffel Tower

Standing 320 m. (1,050 ft.) over Paris, France, the Eiffel Tower was built in 1889 to celebrate the anniversary of the French Revolution of 1789.

The Pyramids

The Pyramids of Giza, which are just outside Cairo in Egypt, were built over 5,000 years ago. These huge monuments were built as tombs for three rulers of ancient Egypt called Khufu, Khafre, and Menkaure.

Great Pyramid
The Pyramid of Khufu is the largest pyramid at Giza. It is 138 m. (451 ft.) high and contains over two million blocks of stone.

Each stone block weighs about 2.25 tonnes (2.5 tons).

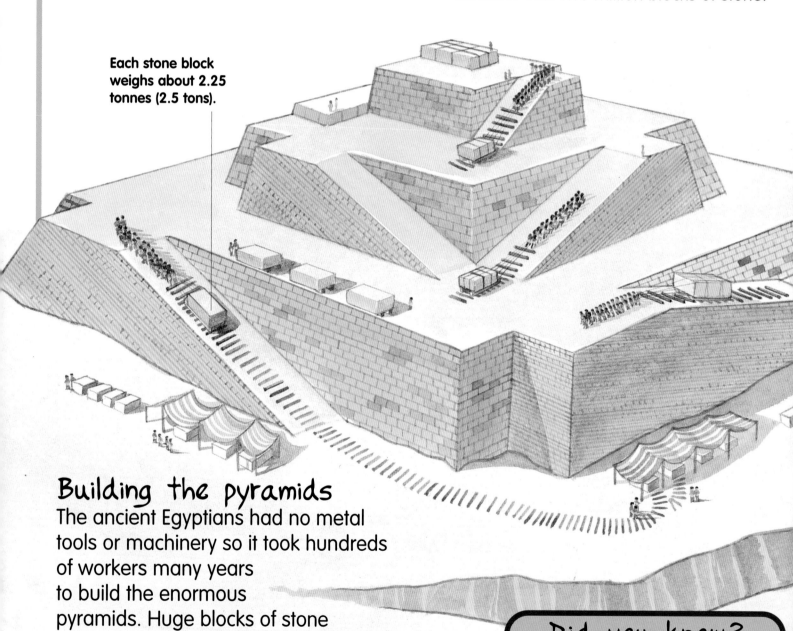

Building the pyramids
The ancient Egyptians had no metal tools or machinery so it took hundreds of workers many years to build the enormous pyramids. Huge blocks of stone were carved from quarries far away and taken by river barge to the site. Here, teams of workers dragged the blocks up to the pyramid itself.

Did you know?
The Pyramid of Khufu is so big that its base would cover ten soccer fields.

8

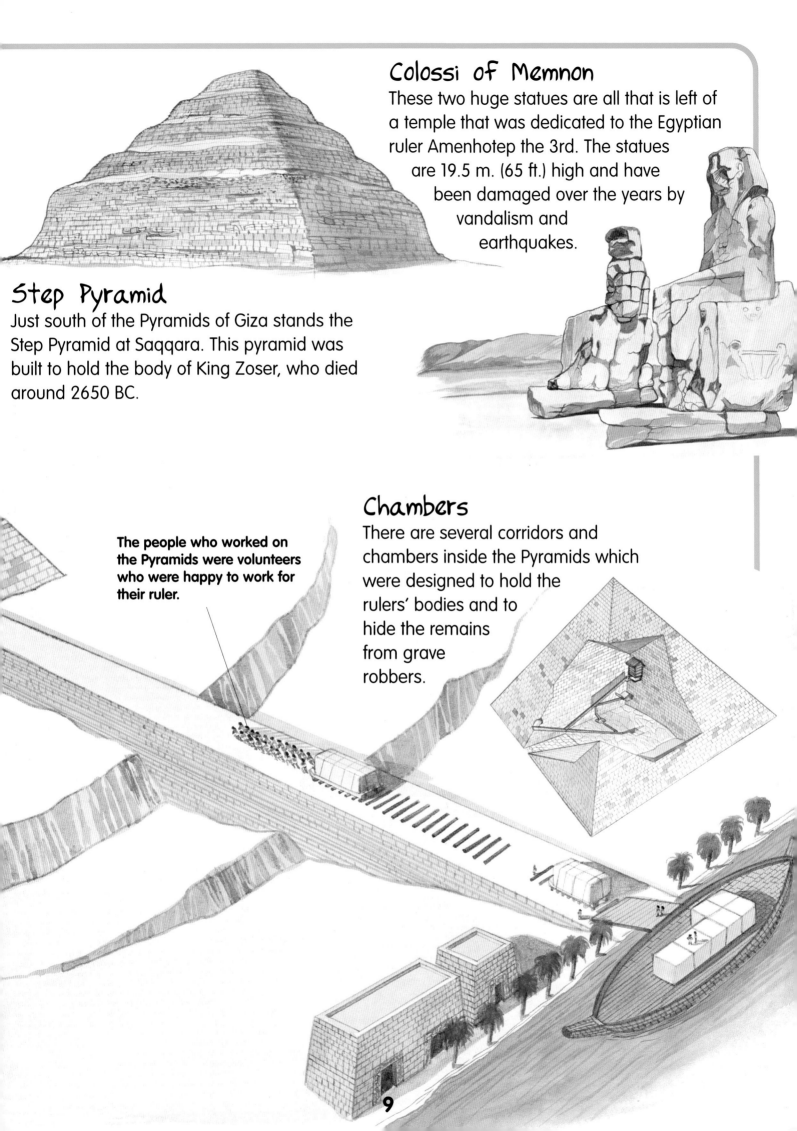

Colossi of Memnon

These two huge statues are all that is left of a temple that was dedicated to the Egyptian ruler Amenhotep the 3rd. The statues are 19.5 m. (65 ft.) high and have been damaged over the years by vandalism and earthquakes.

Step Pyramid

Just south of the Pyramids of Giza stands the Step Pyramid at Saqqara. This pyramid was built to hold the body of King Zoser, who died around 2650 BC.

The people who worked on the Pyramids were volunteers who were happy to work for their ruler.

Chambers

There are several corridors and chambers inside the Pyramids which were designed to hold the rulers' bodies and to hide the remains from grave robbers.

Statue of Liberty

The Statue of Liberty stands above the entrance to New York Harbor, USA. This famous monument of a woman holding a torch was a gift from France to the USA to celebrate the strong relationship between the two countries.

Reaching the top

There are 354 steps inside the statue which lead up to the crown. Beyond this is another staircase which leads up into the torch, the tip of which is 93 m. (305 ft.) above the ground.

Building the statue

The statue was designed by French sculptor Frédéric Auguste Bartholdi. It was put together in Paris, France, between 1870 and 1885. The statue was then dismantled and shipped to New York in 210 crates, before being re-assembled where it stands today.

The outside of the statue is covered in copper which makes it look green.

10

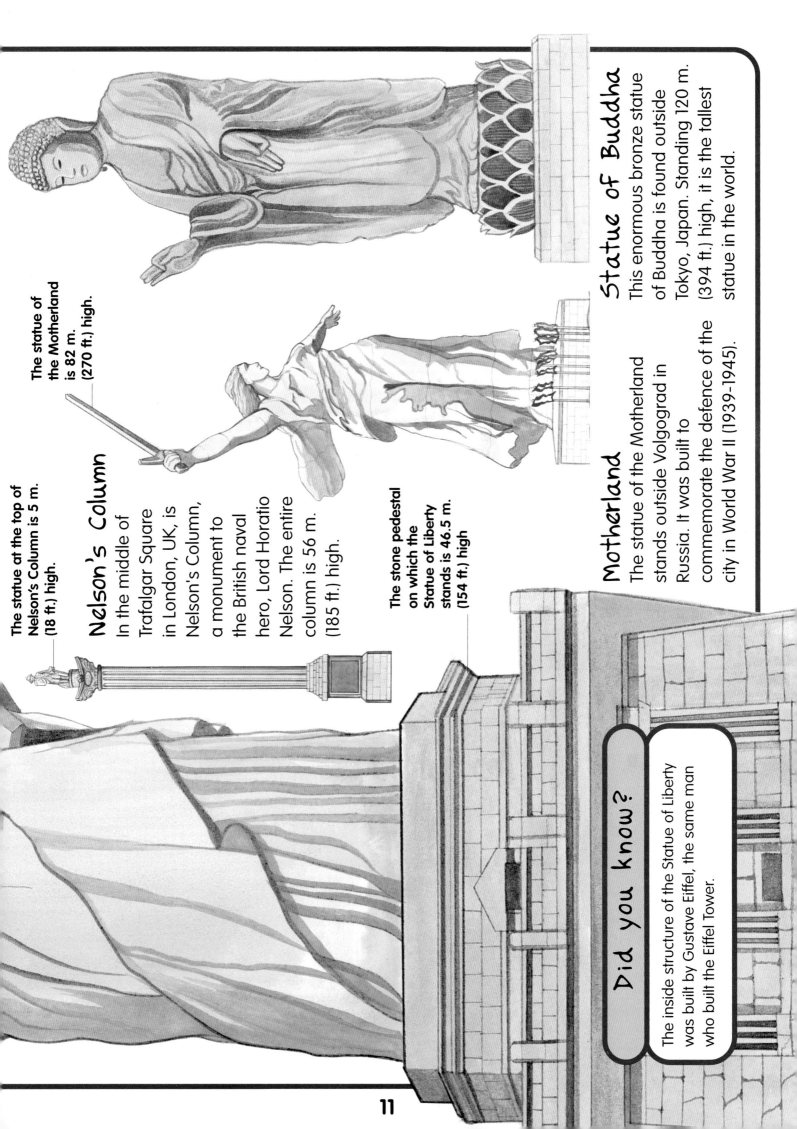

The statue of the Motherland is 82 m. (270 ft.) high.

The statue at the top of Nelson's Column is 5 m. (18 ft.) high.

Nelson's Column

In the middle of Trafalgar Square in London, UK, is Nelson's Column, a monument to the British naval hero, Lord Horatio Nelson. The entire column is 56 m. (185 ft.) high.

The stone pedestal on which the Statue of Liberty stands is 46.5 m. (154 ft.) high

Statue of Buddha

This enormous bronze statue of Buddha is found outside Tokyo, Japan. Standing 120 m. (394 ft.) high, it is the tallest statue in the world.

Motherland

The statue of the Motherland stands outside Volgograd in Russia. It was built to commemorate the defence of the city in World War II (1939-1945).

Did you know?

The inside structure of the Statue of Liberty was built by Gustave Eiffel, the same man who built the Eiffel Tower.

Castles and forts

Before the invention of gunpowder and guns, castles were built to protect people and places from enemy attack. They had to be large and impressive, with strong walls to stop the enemy from getting in.

Himeji Castle's narrow openings were used to fire early guns on attacking troops.

Himeji Castle

This ornate castle was built in Japan during the 1300s. The central white building, called the keep or tenshu, is surrounded by a thick, sloping wall.

Carcassonne

The city of Carcassonne in France is one of the best-preserved fortified cities in the world. The strong walls, built in the 1100s to protect the town from hostile armies, are still visible today.

Edinburgh Castle

Edinburgh Castle stands on an outcrop of volcanic rock, high above the Scottish capital. Three sides of the castle have natural protection from the rock's steep slopes and the fourth side is defended by strong walls and battlements.

Great Wall of China

The Great Wall of China is about 2,400 km. (1,500 miles) long. It stretches from the Mongolian plateau in the west to the Yellow Sea in the east. Building work started on the wall in the third century BC, and continued for another 2,000 years. It was designed to mark the edge of the Chinese empire and to stop invasion. Troops were stationed in towers along the wall and were summoned to areas of trouble by a chain of beacons.

At its highest point, the Great Wall of China is 12 m. (40 ft.) tall.

Did you know?

The Great Wall of China is the only man-made structure that can be seen by astronauts from space.

The Red Fort

Found in the city of Old Delhi in India, the Red Fort was commissioned in the 1600s by Shah Jahan. He was the same man who also had the Taj Mahal built in memory of his wife. This strong fort contains several ornate gardens, as well as barracks and palaces.

The Red Fort gets its name from the red sandstone used to build it.

Tower of London

Construction of the Tower of London, UK, was started in 1087 by King William the 1st, also known as William the Conqueror. Since then, this castle has been used as a safe haven for rulers, a prison for traitors, and a home for the Crown Jewels.

White Tower

In the middle of the castle is the keep, known as the White Tower. This name was first used when King Henry the 3rd had the tower whitewashed during his reign. The White Tower stands 28 m. (92 ft.) high.

Originally, the White Tower was the only building. The baileys were added between 1190 and 1285.

Beefeaters

Ever since the Tower was built, a group of men have kept watch over the buildings. They are called the Yeoman Warders, but their nickname is the "Beefeaters".

The fortifications

Today, the castle has two walls, also called baileys. The inner bailey has 13 towers while the outer bailey has eight towers. Outside these are the remains of a moat.

The Crown Jewels are kept on display in the Jewel House.

Executions

The Tower has been the site of many famous executions, including Sir Thomas More, Lady Jane Grey, and two wives of King Henry the 8th – Anne Boleyn and Catherine Howard.

The White Tower

Prisoners were sometimes brought by boat through this entrance from the River Thames. It is called Traitors' Gate.

Krak des Chevaliers

Krak des Chevaliers (Castle of the Knights) in Syria is often described as the greatest fortress in the world. In the 130 years that it was occupied by crusading knights, the castle walls proved so strong that it was never taken by force.

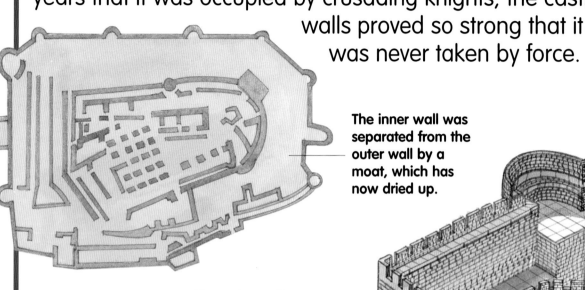

The inner wall was separated from the outer wall by a moat, which has now dried up.

The outer wall had eight towers.

Crusaders and Moors

The Crusaders were a group of Christian knights who journeyed to the Middle East to capture Jerusalem from the Muslims, or Moors, who lived in the region. Krak des Chevaliers was one of the last castles to be captured from the Crusaders. The Muslims finally tricked the Crusaders by forging a note from the knights' leader telling them to surrender the castle to the Moors!

Crusader   **Moor**

The storerooms at Krak des Chevaliers held enough weapons and supplies to last for five years.

Inside the castle

Krak des Chevaliers was extremely well supplied. It had its own water supply, barns for storing grain, and comfortable rooms and halls. It even had its own windmill for grinding flour.

The knights would assemble in the Great Hall.

Strong walls

The walls of Krak des Chevaliers were very strong. Legend has it that the Muslim leader, Saladin, marched an army up to the castle, but called off the attack when he saw all the fortifications.

17

Palaces and parliaments

Government buildings and palaces play important roles in society. They are a country's seat of power, where the nation's rulers meet to make new laws. As a result, these buildings are large and impressive places.

Victoria Tower is used to store over two million documents.

Palace of Westminster

The Palace of Westminster in London, UK, is also known as the Houses of Parliament. It is home to the parliament of the United Kingdom.

White House

Since 1800, the White House in Washington D.C., USA, has been the official home of the President of the United States of America. It is also a major tourist attraction and over 1.5 million people tour this building every year.

Alhambra

Built between 1238 and 1358, the Alhambra in Spain was a palace and fortress for the Moorish rulers from North Africa. The castle contains several ornate gardens and courts that are richly decorated with fountains and tiles.

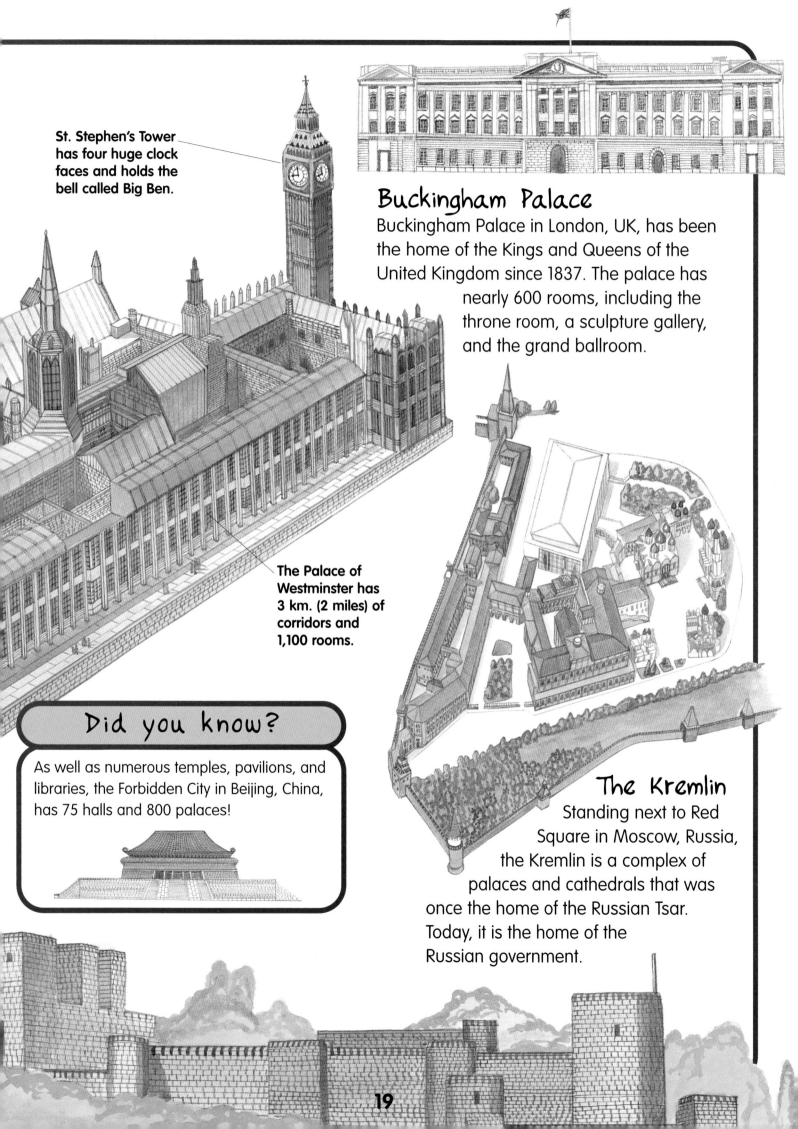

St. Stephen's Tower has four huge clock faces and holds the bell called Big Ben.

The Palace of Westminster has 3 km. (2 miles) of corridors and 1,100 rooms.

Buckingham Palace

Buckingham Palace in London, UK, has been the home of the Kings and Queens of the United Kingdom since 1837. The palace has nearly 600 rooms, including the throne room, a sculpture gallery, and the grand ballroom.

Did you know?

As well as numerous temples, pavilions, and libraries, the Forbidden City in Beijing, China, has 75 halls and 800 palaces!

The Kremlin

Standing next to Red Square in Moscow, Russia, the Kremlin is a complex of palaces and cathedrals that was once the home of the Russian Tsar. Today, it is the home of the Russian government.

19

Palace of Versailles

The Palace of Versailles lies just outside the French capital of Paris. It started off as a hunting lodge for the French rulers, but was transformed into Europe's largest palace by King Louis the 14th.

Louis the 14th was known as the Sun King.

The Sun King

Louis the 14th ruled France from 1643 to 1715. His reign was remarkable for the glittering court at Versailles. He also oversaw many other building works, including the completion of the Louvre in Paris.

This is known as the Fountain of Neptune.

Courtyard gate

Fountains and gardens

Behind the palace are the huge gardens of Versailles. These contain ponds and fountains as well as the Grand Canal.

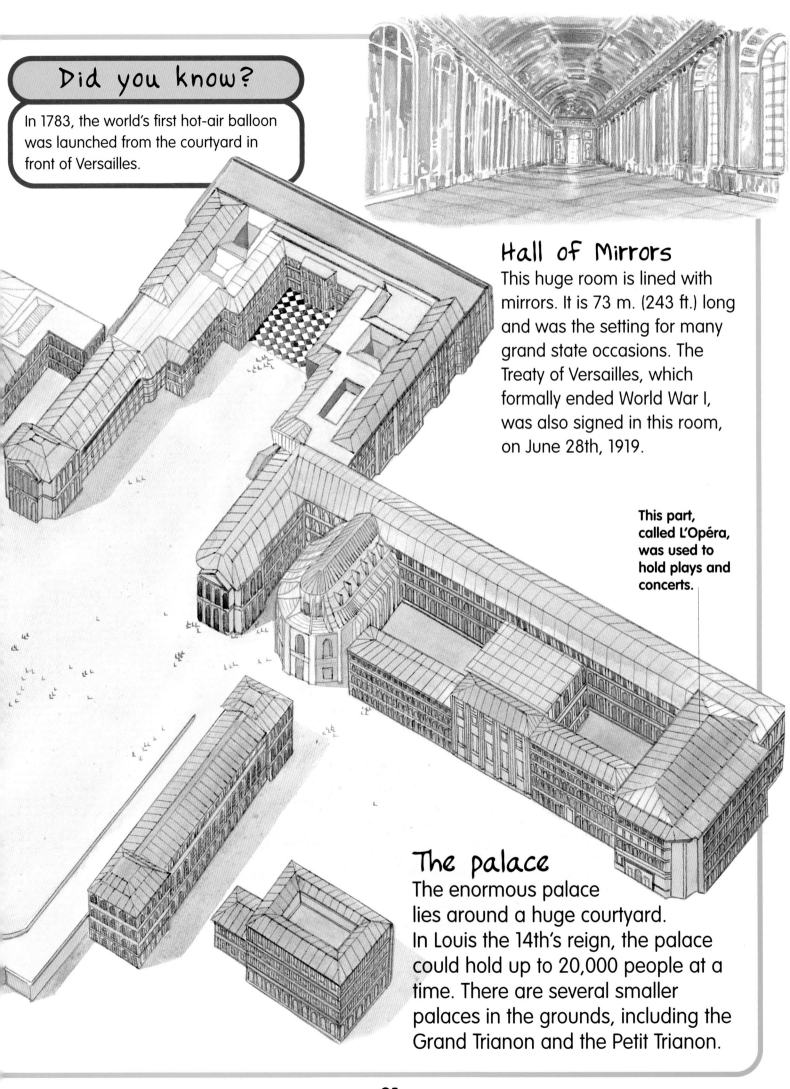

Did you know?

In 1783, the world's first hot-air balloon was launched from the courtyard in front of Versailles.

Hall of Mirrors

This huge room is lined with mirrors. It is 73 m. (243 ft.) long and was the setting for many grand state occasions. The Treaty of Versailles, which formally ended World War I, was also signed in this room, on June 28th, 1919.

This part, called L'Opéra, was used to hold plays and concerts.

The palace

The enormous palace lies around a huge courtyard. In Louis the 14th's reign, the palace could hold up to 20,000 people at a time. There are several smaller palaces in the grounds, including the Grand Trianon and the Petit Trianon.

Homes and houses

Since the dawn of time, people have needed somewhere to live. The very earliest shelters were caves. However, these were not always in the right place, so people learnt how to build their own homes. Over the years these homes have become more sophisticated, comfortable, and varied.

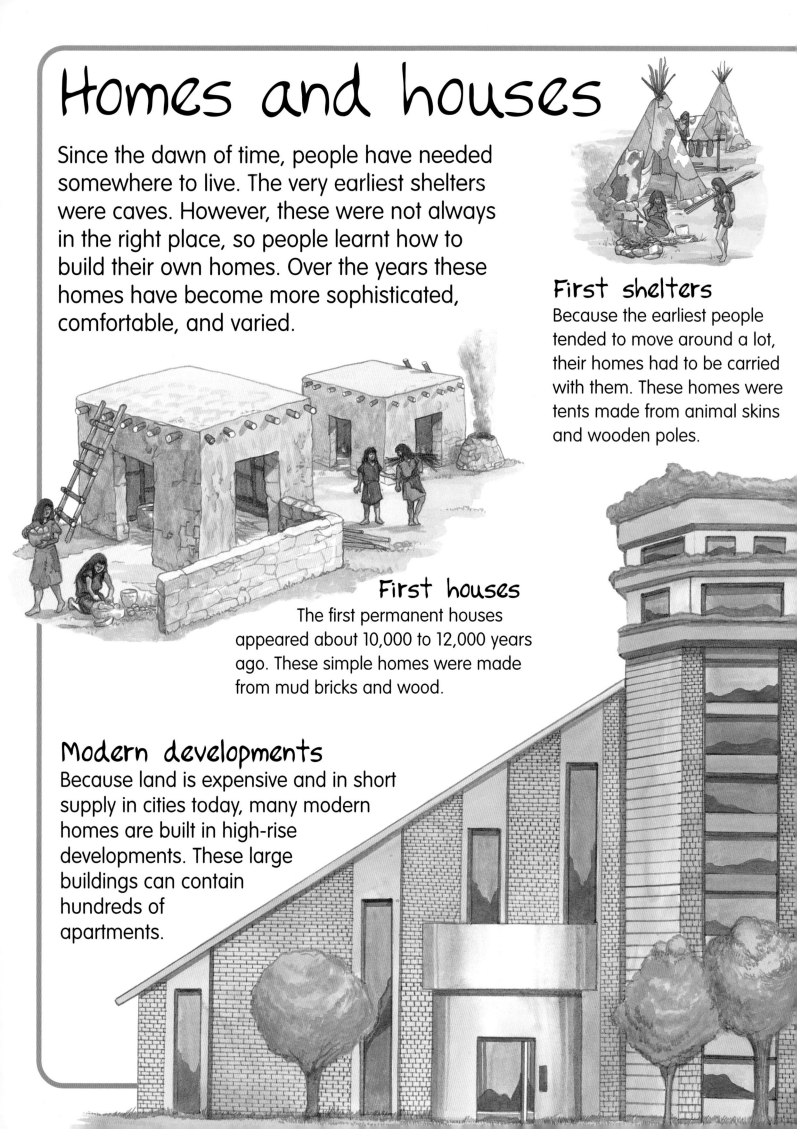

First shelters

Because the earliest people tended to move around a lot, their homes had to be carried with them. These homes were tents made from animal skins and wooden poles.

First houses

The first permanent houses appeared about 10,000 to 12,000 years ago. These simple homes were made from mud bricks and wood.

Modern developments

Because land is expensive and in short supply in cities today, many modern homes are built in high-rise developments. These large buildings can contain hundreds of apartments.

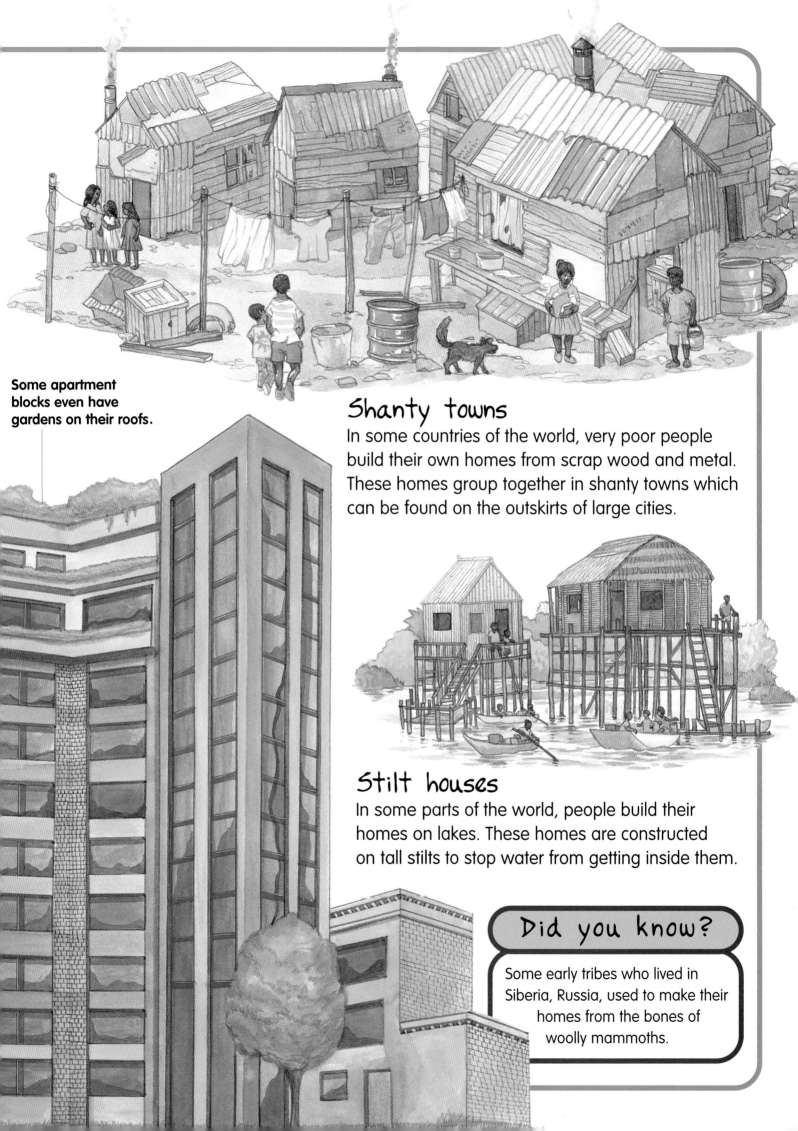

Some apartment blocks even have gardens on their roofs.

Shanty towns

In some countries of the world, very poor people build their own homes from scrap wood and metal. These homes group together in shanty towns which can be found on the outskirts of large cities.

Stilt houses

In some parts of the world, people build their homes on lakes. These homes are constructed on tall stilts to stop water from getting inside them.

Did you know?

Some early tribes who lived in Siberia, Russia, used to make their homes from the bones of woolly mammoths.

Roman homes

The Romans ruled a huge area of Europe and North Africa about 2,000 years ago. They constructed many large and impressive buildings, including homes, aqueducts, temples, and palaces.

Decoration

Many Roman homes were richly decorated with frescoes painted on the walls and mosaics on the floors.

Fresco

Mosaic

Apartment blocks

Many Romans were not rich enough to afford their own villa. Instead, they had to live in small apartments in the cities.

The villa

The wealthiest families in the Roman Empire were able to live in comfort and style inside large villas, surrounded by farms. Many Roman farms were small, but some of the bigger farms needed hundreds of slaves to work on them.

Did you know?

Some Roman houses had a simple form of central heating system called a hypocaust, where heated air flowed under the floors.

City life

City apartments were cramped and many were built above shops. These densely packed buildings often caught fire. However, the Romans had their own emergency services to fight these blazes!

Roman villas had pools of water which helped to cool the air.

A Roman surveyor checked that the road ran in a straight line.

Roman roads

The Romans built straight roads to link their homes and cities. The base of each road was made from sand and pebbles. The top was made from large stones and was slightly curved so that rainwater drained away.

Places of entertainment

People have always built special places in which they can be entertained. These places range from small, intimate theatres for plays and concerts to enormous sports stadia that can hold over 100,000 people.

Greek theatre

Some of the earliest places of entertainment were theatres, built by the ancient Greeks over 2,000 years ago. They were usually cut into the side of a hill so that everyone in the audience could see the stage.

The Mayans' ball game was called pok-ta-pok.

Mayan ball court

The Mayan civilization flourished in Central America over 1,000 years ago. They used to play a ball game on a huge court. Players used their elbows, knees, and hips to send a ball through hoops on the sides of the court.

The Globe

The original Globe Theatre stood in London, UK, during the 1600s. Many of William Shakespeare's plays were first performed here. The Globe was recently restored, complete with authentic open-air seating and a thatched roof.

Crystal Palace

The Crystal Palace was built in 1851 to hold the Great Exhibition in London, UK. It was made entirely of iron and glass and was 563 m. (1,848 ft.) long and 124 m. (408 ft.) wide.

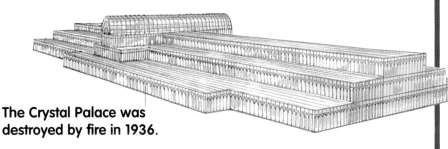

The Crystal Palace was destroyed by fire in 1936.

Did you know?

The Crystal Palace could hold an area equivalent to 18 soccer fields!

Sydney Opera House

Opened in 1973, the Opera House in Sydney, Australia, is one of the most beautiful buildings in the world. Underneath its sail-like roofs are several halls, including a 1,547-seat opera hall and a 2,679-seat concert hall.

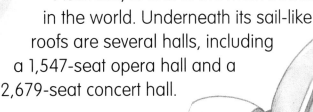

Stadium

Massive dome stadia are becoming more common. These structures can seat up to 60,000 people for pop concerts and sports events, and some have roofs that can slide back.

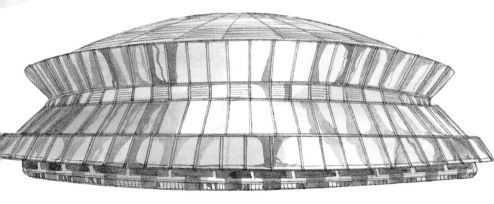

The Colosseum

When it was completed in AD80, the Colosseum in Rome, Italy, was the largest Roman amphitheatre. It was built to hold gladiator fights and other spectacles, including mock battles and animal fights.

In the shade
Around the top of the Colosseum were some 240 poles. These supported a huge canvas awning, called the velarium, which shaded the crowd from the Sun.

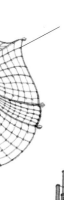

This gladiator is fighting with a net and a trident.

Gladiators
Gladiators were trained fighters who had been prisoners, criminals, or slaves. They usually fought each other to the death using different weapons, including swords, nets, and tridents.

Sea battles
The Colosseum is an amphitheatre. In this type of building the audience sits in a circle around the arena. Sometimes, the floor of the Colosseum's arena was flooded to stage realistic sea battles.

Did you know?

The real name for the Colosseum is the Flavian Amphitheatre. It was called the Colosseum because a colossal statue of the Roman Emperor Nero used to stand nearby.

Each chariot race lasted for seven laps of the Circus Maximus.

Circus Maximus

Not far from the Colosseum in Rome are the remains of the Circus Maximus. This huge arena was built around 600BC and could hold up to 300,000 people who came to watch the chariot races.

The velarium was operated by sailors from the nearby port of Ostia.

Underground

Underneath the Colosseum was a complicated maze of rooms and tunnels where gladiators and prisoners waited before going to fight. Animals, including lions and tigers, were also kept here and then released into the arena through special trap doors and elevators.

The Colosseum could seat between 40,000 and 70,000 people.

Churches and temples

Throughout history, churches and temples have been important buildings. These structures can cover huge areas and some are even decorated in solid gold!

These statues are 20 m. (65 ft.) high.

Temple of Ramses the 2nd

This temple was built by the ancient Egyptians over three thousand years ago. Between 1960 and 1968, the temple was moved to stop it from being flooded by a lake.

Golden Temple

This shiny temple is in the city of Amritsar in India. Its roof is actually covered with gold.

These tall towers are called minarets.

Angkor Wat has many elaborate carvings, including one which is 50 m. (160ft.) long.

Angkor Wat

The main temple in the ruined city of Angkor in Cambodia is the largest religious building in the world. It is one of nearly 300 temples in the city which was built over 800 years ago.

Haggia Sophia

This building is in the Turkish city of Istanbul. It started life as a Christian church, but was converted into an Islamic mosque 500 years ago.

The sacred black stone found in the Great Mosque at Mecca is thought to have been a meteorite that crashed to Earth from space.

Muslim pilgrims walk around and kiss the sacred stone which sits under a black shroud.

Mecca

The Great Mosque at Mecca in Saudi Arabia is the most sacred site of the Islamic religion. Every year, millions of people come here on pilgrimage. The Mosque itself can hold up to 300,000 people at one time.

The towers of the Sagrada Familia are 135 m. (450 ft.) tall.

Sagrada Familia

This church is in Barcelona, Spain. Work was started on the cathedral in 1882 and is still going on, over 100 years later. Much of the work was overseen by the Spanish architect Antonio Gaudi. He also built many other fantastically shaped buildings throughout Barcelona.

St. Paul's Cathedral

After the original St. Paul's Cathedral was destroyed in the Great Fire of London in 1666, the city commissioned architect Sir Christopher Wren to build a replacement. The new cathedral was started in 1675 and took 35 years to complete.

Did you know?

The Whispering Gallery in the dome of St. Paul's is so called because a whisper against one wall of the gallery can be heard on the opposite wall 33 m. (110 ft.) away!

The dome is 34 m. (112 ft.) wide.

North transept

Dome
The dome of St. Paul's reaches a height of 108 m. (356 ft.). On top of this is a golden ball and cross which were added in 1708 and replaced in 1821.

Nave

Around St. Paul's
As with many other churches and cathedrals, St. Paul's was built in the shape of a cross. The longest part is called the nave. Directly opposite the nave is the choir, and there are the south and north transepts on either side of these. Underneath the cathedral is the crypt which holds the graves and memorials of many famous people including Sir Christopher Wren and Sir Alexander Fleming.

The Great West door at the entrance to the nave is 9 m. (30 ft.) tall.

The ball and cross on top of St. Paul's are 7 m. (23 ft.) high and weigh 7 tonnes (8 tons).

Choir

Our Lady of Peace

The Basilica of Our Lady of Peace in the Ivory Coast, Africa, is the largest church in the world. The dome of the basilica is 158 m. (519 ft.) high and the church can seat nearly 7,000 people.

The south transept contains the memorials of several British heroes, including Lord Horatio Nelson and Captain Robert Scott.

The dome of St. Peter's is 120 m. (400 ft.) high.

St. Peter's

The Basilica of St. Peter's in Rome, Italy, took 120 years to complete. The dome that sits on top was designed by the artist Michelangelo. Directly under the dome is the tomb of St. Peter.

Industrial buildings

They may not be beautiful to look at, but industrial buildings play vital roles. They provide us with energy, help us to find oil, and even contain rockets that go into space.

Oil platform

Some oil deposits lie under the ocean floor. To reach these, huge oil platforms are needed. Some of these have enormous supporting legs that stretch right down to the sea floor.

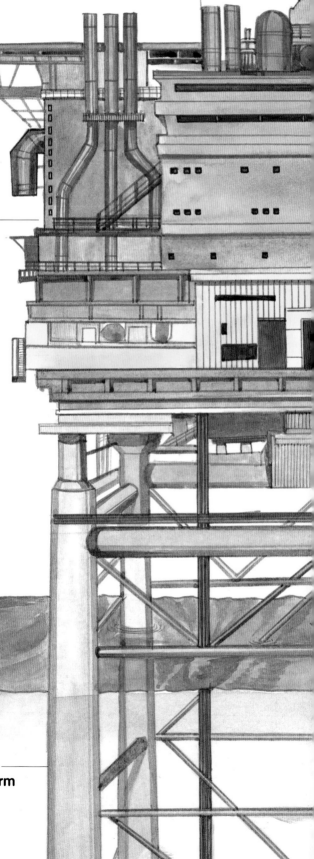

Oil platforms can be home to more than 100 crew members.

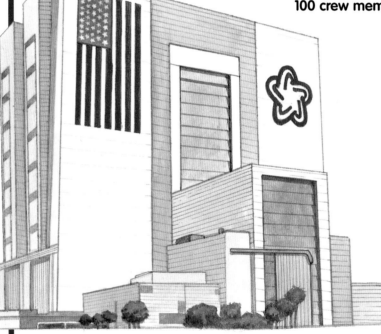

Vehicle Assembly Building

The Vehicle Assembly Building at Cape Canaveral in Florida, USA, is where NASA puts together the rockets it sends into space. It was used to build the enormous Saturn V rockets that took people to the Moon and is now used to hold the Space Shuttle.

The supporting legs anchor the oil platform in place.

Nuclear reactor

Huge nuclear reactors provide power for millions of people around the world. Inside them, nuclear fuel is used to create electricity.

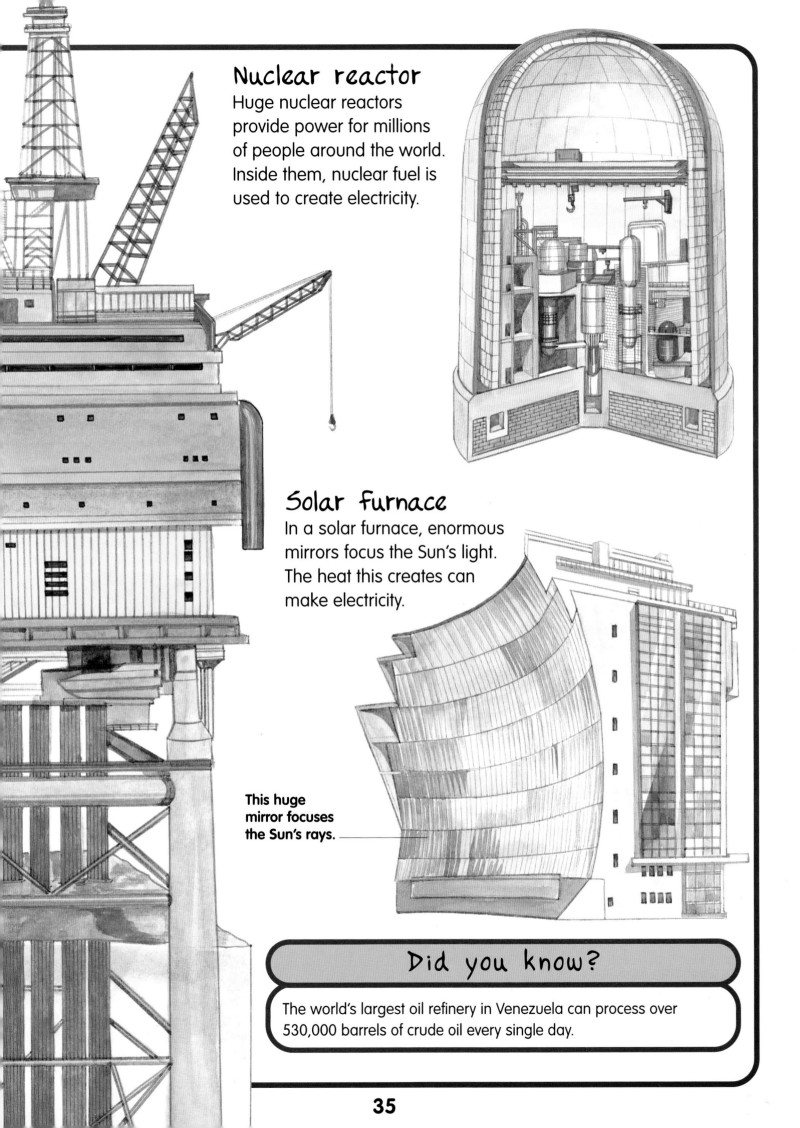

Solar furnace

In a solar furnace, enormous mirrors focus the Sun's light. The heat this creates can make electricity.

This huge mirror focuses the Sun's rays.

Did you know?

The world's largest oil refinery in Venezuela can process over 530,000 barrels of crude oil every single day.

Hydroelectric dam

Water has always been very important for human society. It has helped our crops grow and has driven our mills for thousands of years. We can now use water to create electricity to power our homes, schools, and work places.

Water wheel

Water wheels are driven by flowing water to pow machinery. They also lift water into irrigation channels, where it can be carried to crops.

Hoover Dam

The Hoover Dam in the USA was completed in 1937. It supplies power, drinking water, flood control, and irrigation. The dam has created a lake that is 185 km. (115 miles) long.

Did you know?

The Dinorwig hydroelectric power station in Great Britain is actually a hollowed-out mountain.

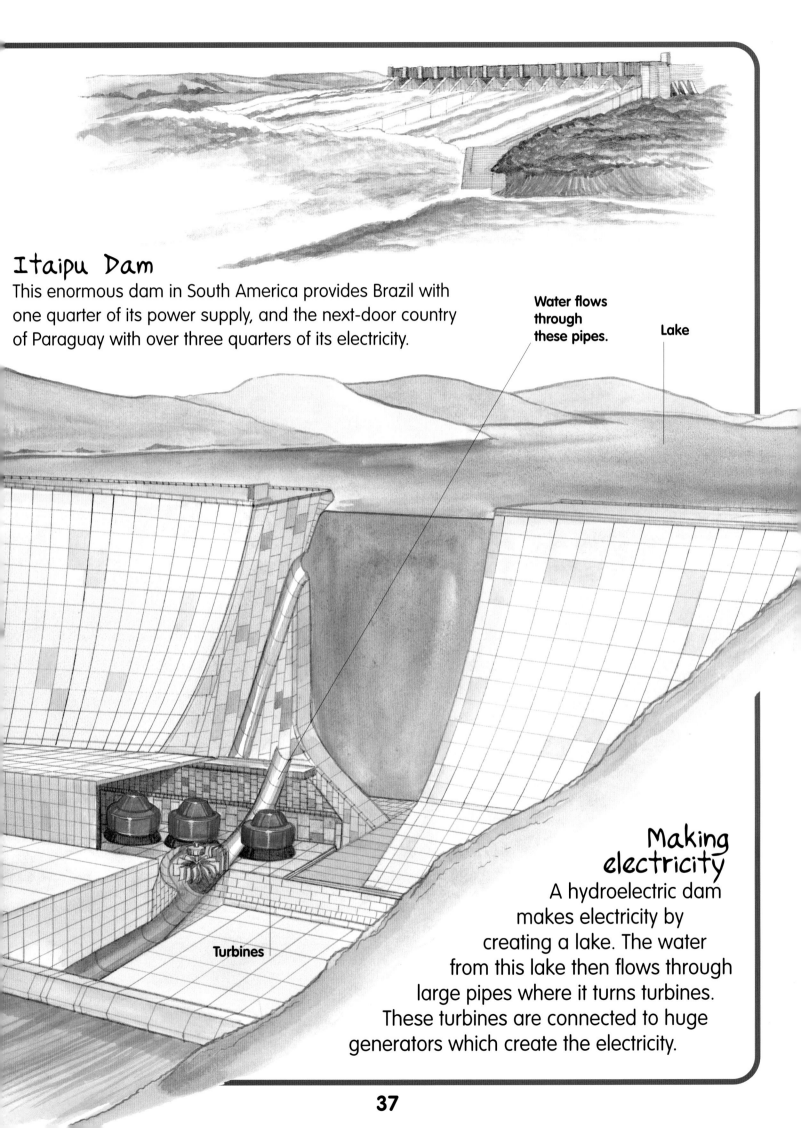

Itaipu Dam
This enormous dam in South America provides Brazil with one quarter of its power supply, and the next-door country of Paraguay with over three quarters of its electricity.

Water flows through these pipes.

Lake

Turbines

Making electricity
A hydroelectric dam makes electricity by creating a lake. The water from this lake then flows through large pipes where it turns turbines. These turbines are connected to huge generators which create the electricity.

Buildings for travel

Getting from one place to another requires a lot of building work. Roads and railways make the journey easier, and these need bridges and tunnels to take them over or through obstacles. You also need buildings at the start and end of journeys, such as railway stations or airports.

Did you know?

The ceiling of Grand Central Station is decorated with 2,500 stars showing the constellations of the night sky.

Viaduct

Famed for their road building, the Romans were also very good at building bridges to carry these roads over valleys and rivers. These bridges are called viaducts.

Pont de Normandie

The Pont de Normandie connects the French towns of Le Havre and Honfleur. It is called a cable-stayed bridge because the weight of the bridge is supported by the thick cables and the tall pylons.

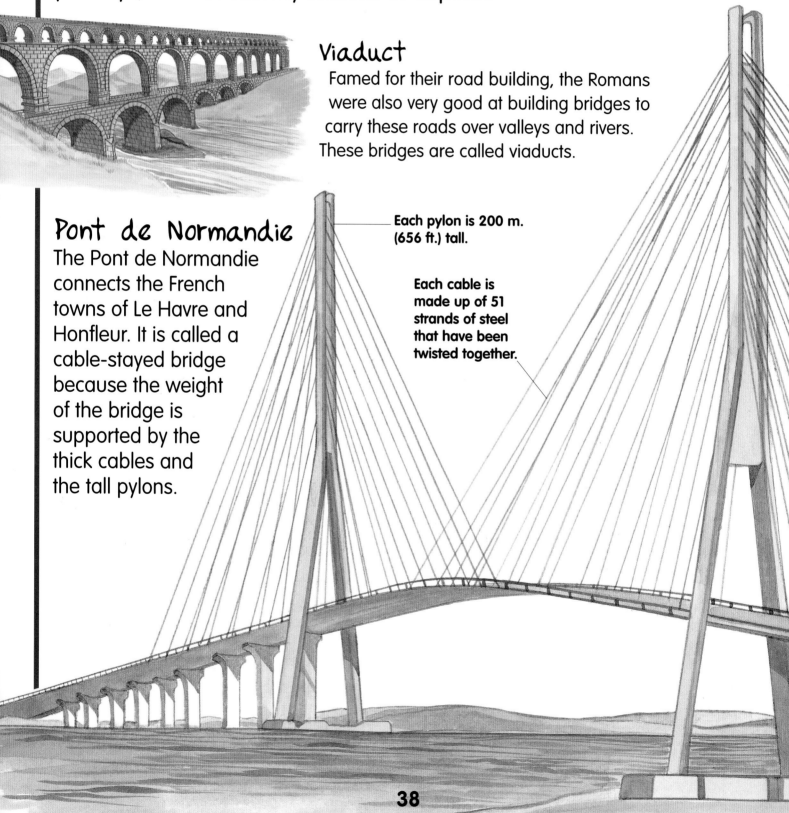

Each pylon is 200 m. (656 ft.) tall.

Each cable is made up of 51 strands of steel that have been twisted together.

38

Ellis Island

Ellis Island in New York Harbor was the immigration station for people arriving in the United States. About 17 million people passed through the facility between 1892 and 1943.

Tower Bridge

Tower Bridge in London, UK, was completed in 1894 after taking eight years to build. In its first month alone, the bridge was raised 655 times. Today, river traffic is not as busy, but the bridge is still raised about 500 times a year.

Grand Central

Grand Central Station is a railway station in the middle of New York City, USA. Over 100 million people pass through the station every year.

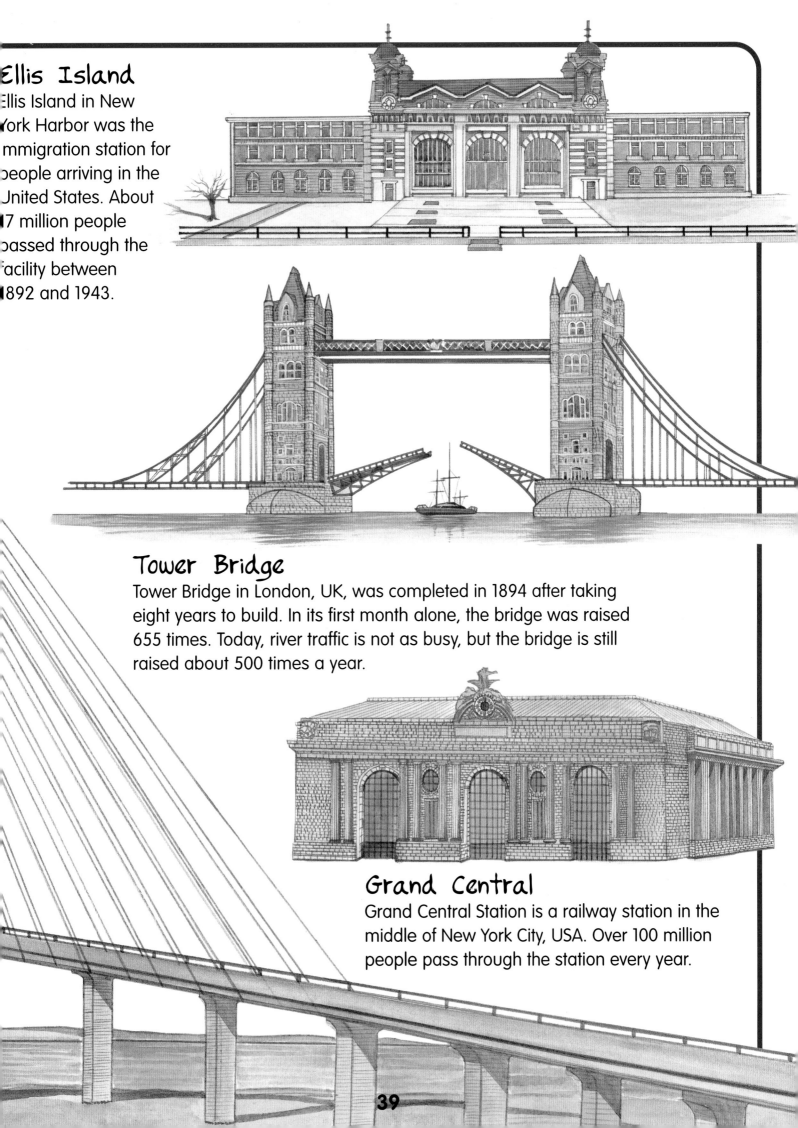

Kansai Airport

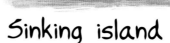

Kansai Airport is found on an artificial island 3 km. (2 miles) off the coast of Japan. Engineers had to make sure that the island could survive the earthquakes and typhoons that occur frequently in the area. Since its opening in 1994, the airport has handled over 150,000 flights every year.

Sinking island

Problems occurred at Kansai Airport when it was discovered that the artificial island was sinking at a rate of 5 cm. (2 in.) every month! More earth had to be added in an attempt to stop the island from disappearing into the sea.

Did you know?

While building Kansai Airport, engineers had to flatten three mountains to provide debris to make the artificial island.

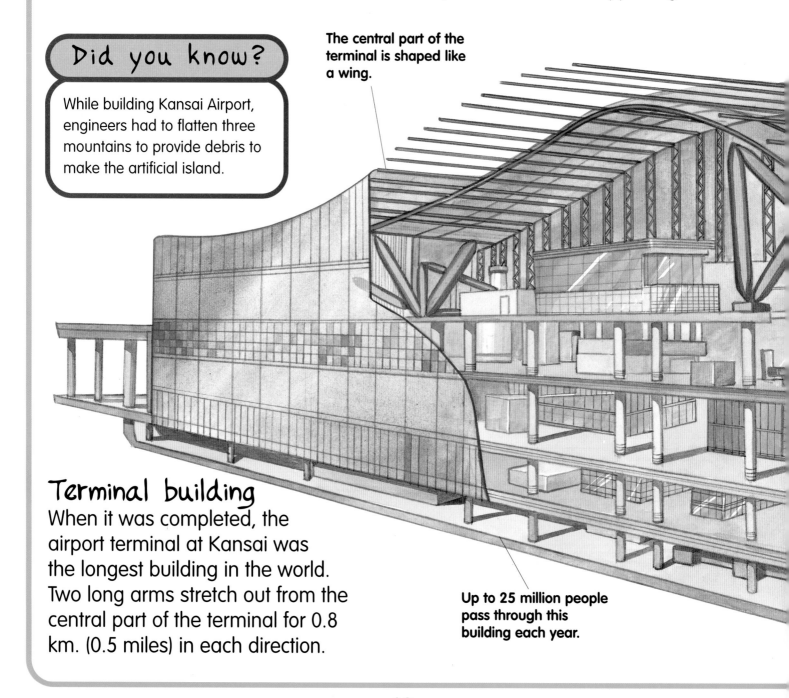

The central part of the terminal is shaped like a wing.

Up to 25 million people pass through this building each year.

Terminal building

When it was completed, the airport terminal at Kansai was the longest building in the world. Two long arms stretch out from the central part of the terminal for 0.8 km. (0.5 miles) in each direction.

Chep Lak Kok
Another airport found on an artificial island is Chep Lak Kok in Hong Kong, China. The island covers an enormous 8 sq. km. (3 sq. miles).

Los Angeles International
One of the strangest looking airport buildings is the former air traffic control building at Los Angeles International Airport. Today, this mushroom-shaped building has been converted into an unusual restaurant.

There are 41 gates at Kansai Airport.

41

Skyscrapers

Look into the sky the next time you are in a city and you will see huge buildings stretching up above you. They are called skyscrapers.

Did you know?

The proposed Millennium Tower in Tokyo, Japan, will be nearly twice as tall as the Petronas Towers, if it is completed.

The pod of the CN Tower has a restaurant, a nightclub, and observation decks.

The Flatiron Building has 21 floors and is 87 m. (285 ft.) tall.

The two Petronas Towers are linked by a bridge half-way up.

Flatiron Building

Older skyscrapers, such as the Flatiron Building in New York, USA, could not be very tall because the buildings weren't strong enough.

The Chrysler Building, completed in 1930, was the world's tallest building for just a few months until the Empire State Building was finished.

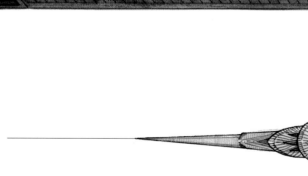
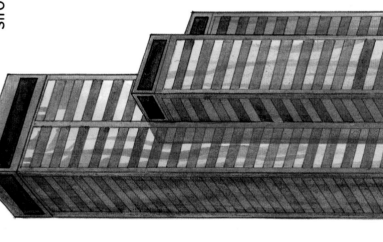

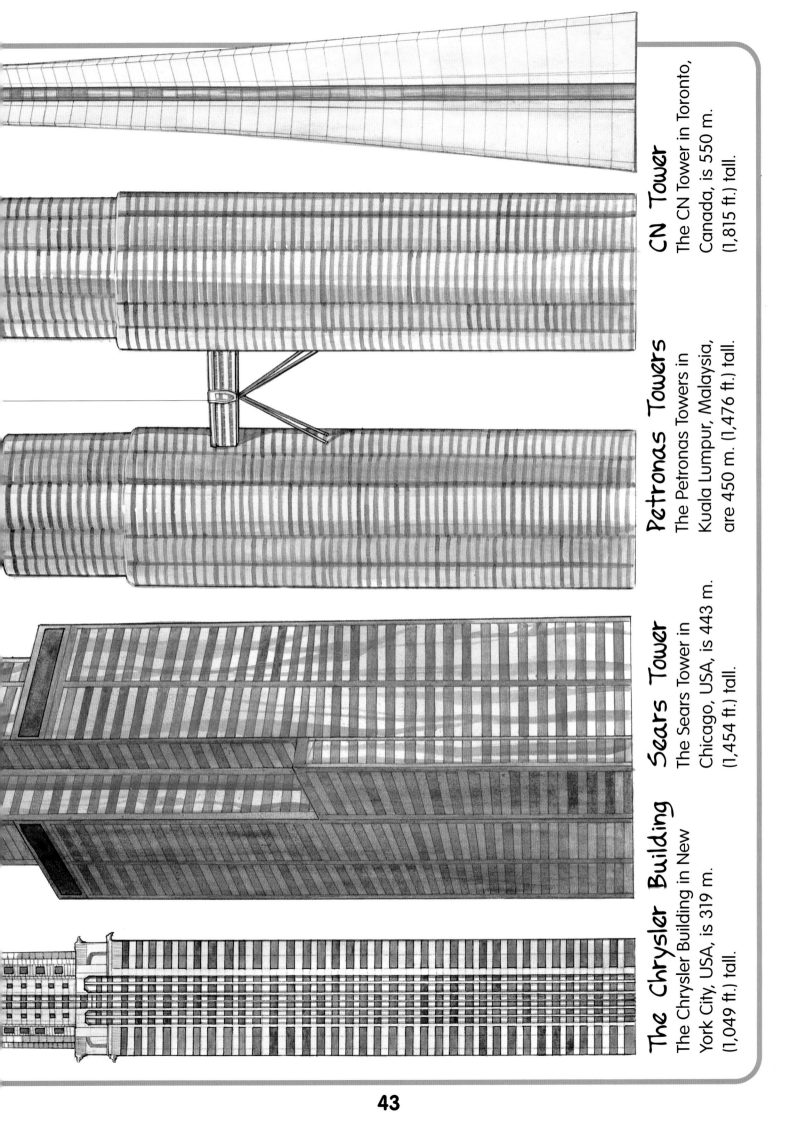

CN Tower
The CN Tower in Toronto, Canada, is 550 m. (1,815 ft.) tall.

Petronas Towers
The Petronas Towers in Kuala Lumpur, Malaysia, are 450 m. (1,476 ft.) tall.

Sears Tower
The Sears Tower in Chicago, USA, is 443 m. (1,454 ft.) tall.

The Chrysler Building
The Chrysler Building in New York City, USA, is 319 m. (1,049 ft.) tall.

Empire State Building

The tip of the Empire State Building's radio mast is 443 m. (1,454 ft.) above the ground.

Empire Facts

The Empire State Building has 73 elevators that travel up and down 11 km. (7 miles) of shafts. There are 1,860 steps up to the 102nd floor. 90 tonnes (100 tons) of rubbish is removed from the building each month, which is made by the 850 companies and the 15,000 people who work there.

Towering above the other skyscrapers on Manhattan Island in New York, USA, is the Empire State Building. It was completed in 1931 and held the record as the world's tallest building for over 40 years.

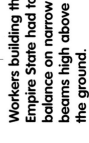

Workers building the Empire State had to balance on narrow beams high above the ground.

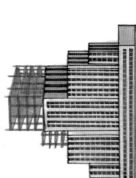

Fast building

The Empire State was built astonishingly quickly for such a tall building. All 102 floors were completed in just one year and 45 days.

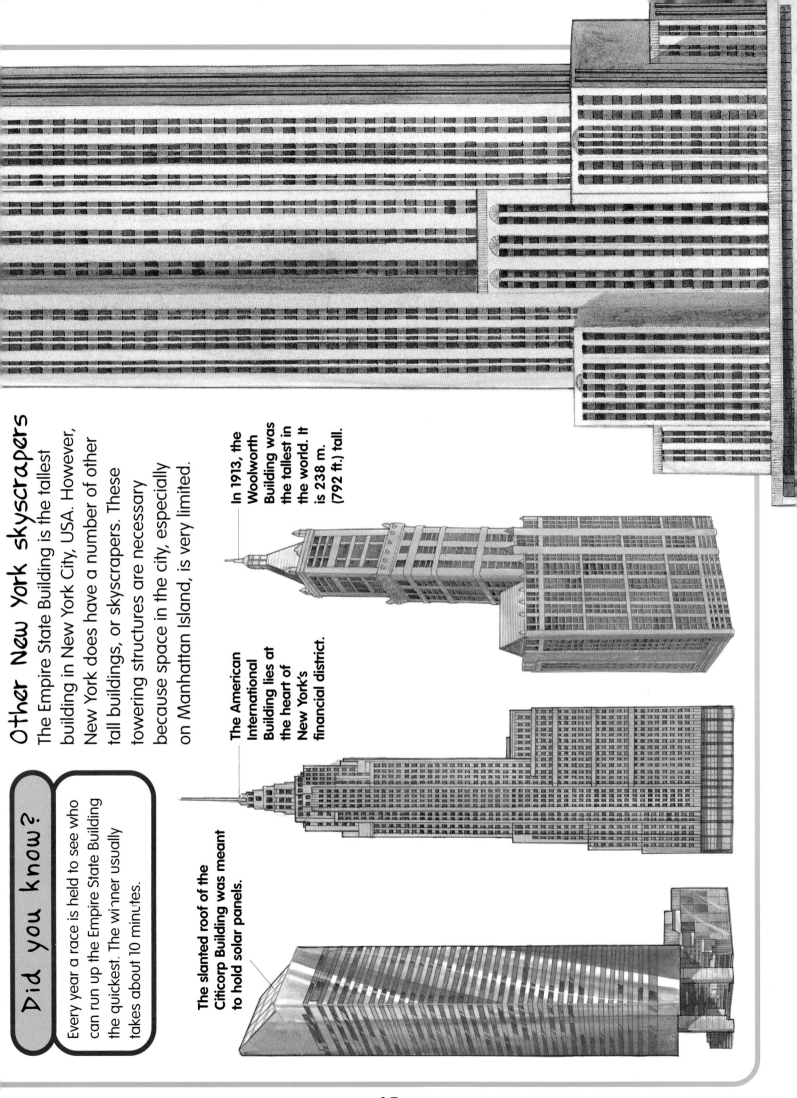

Other New York skyscrapers

The Empire State Building is the tallest building in New York City, USA. However, New York does have a number of other tall buildings, or skyscrapers. These towering structures are necessary because space in the city, especially on Manhattan Island, is very limited.

In 1913, the Woolworth Building was the tallest in the world. It is 238 m. (792 ft.) tall.

The American International Building lies at the heart of New York's financial district.

The slanted roof of the Citicorp Building was meant to hold solar panels.

Did you know?

Every year a race is held to see who can run up the Empire State Building the quickest. The winner usually takes about 10 minutes.

Glossary

Apartment
A room or number of rooms in a larger building for a person or family to live in.

Bailey
The bailey is the fortified wall that surrounds a castle keep.

Basilica
A Roman Catholic church that has special ceremonial rights.

Cable-stayed bridge
A type of suspension bridge in which the supporting cables are connected directly to the bridge deck.

Cathedral
This is the largest church in a religious area which is called the diocese. The cathedral contains the official throne of the bishop.

Choir
The part of a church found in front of the altar. It is lined with benches that are used by the singers (who are also called the choir!) and the clergy.

Crypt
A crypt is a cellar or underground chamber beneath a building. The crypts in churches are usually used to hold the remains and monuments of dead people.

Fresco
A type of wall painting in which the picture is painted directly onto the wall while the plaster is still wet.

Keep
The main tower in a castle or fortress.